OUR GOD
GENOME

OUR GOD GENOME

The Reflections of Humanities Belief Systems

Richard H. Moore

WillMoor Vision LLC
Cedar Hill, TX

WillMoor Vision LLC

Published by:
WillMoor Vision LLC 445 East FM 1382 Suite 3 PBM 705
Cedar Hill, TX 75104
Tel.: 972.754.8455
www.willmoorvision.com

ISBN-13: 9781508890737
ISBN-10: 1508890730
Jacket design by Hubert Moore

Attention colleges and universities, corporations and churches, and other organizations: Quantity discounts are available on bulk purchases of this book for educational training purposes, fund-raising, or gift giving. Special books, booklets, or book excerpts can be created to fit your specific needs. Inquiries on speaking engagements contact lll Ink Entertainment at lllinkentetainment@gmail.com. For more information contact WillMoor Vision LLC.at willmoorvision@gmail.com see www.willmoorvision.com

Printed in the United States of America

TABLE OF CONTENTS

DEDICATION AND ACKNOWLEDGEMENTS

I dedicate this book to my lovely and beautiful wife Darlene Marie, who is my encourager, counselor, supporter and most of all, my best friend for 37 years.

To my daughters, LaShundra R Moore, LaStassia M Williams and her husband Damien Williams, and Ebony L Moore. Also my wonderful grandchildren, Chrischen Irvin, and Jernecia, Payton, Paige and Parker Williams.

In special memory of my earthly father, Harrel Moore Sr., who taught me how grand and great God is; my mother, Thelma M Moore, who taught me the importance of commitment to an organized church of righteous believers; and to my father in the ministry, Bishop Nash Wilson, who brought me to the recognition and acceptance of my calling as a preacher of the Gospel.

In addition, I like to acknowledge Dr. Howard E. Anderson Sr. (Sr. Pastor of the "Exciting" Singing Hills Baptist Church), and thank the graduate school professors, of the master's program where I attended, who have directed me in the reflective papers which has formulated this book.

Finally, it is with extreme thankfulness and acknowledgement of God's Holy Spirit for His guiding presence and guarding power in providing me with the information, knowledge, and spiritual insight to complete this book.

INTRODUCTION
REFLECTION OF HUMANITY

Within our life span, we humans, for the most part, would like to be recognized for something that we have achieved or have proudly produced without having to fabricate the purpose or meaning. These references in our life give each one of us a sense of belonging, a sense of understanding our existence, and a level of excitement. No person is immune to this emotional reality, not even the worse person on this planet. Not all of us try to be famous, but we would like to be recognized by someone, either by family, friend, organization, or coworkers; large or small. Even though some of us have been recognized to a large degree, we are sometimes left wondering, was that all to it, or is there something more? But there are some people who want a larger understanding of themselves and the world around them, so they may ask broader questions like, who are we; what defines us; and what are we known for doing best? Well in my estimation, we are who we are, we are defined by our actions, and we are known by the works that we do. Let me give you a short synopsis about myself.

My name is Richard H Moore; I am an African American male; a Preacher of the Gospel of Christ; and a married man who loves his wife and family. Previously

I have worked as a warehouse worker, print shop manager, warehouse manager, and computer operator for different fortune 500 corporations. I am and have worked as a visual artist and author of a children's book over my thirty plus working years. Now for those who know me personally, know I am a history, science fiction, and sports buff. My favorite channels on TV are the History channel, the Science channel, the Syfy channel, and the sports channel. And there are still parts of me that are not mentioned, but in everything previously mentioned about me, a portion of my personality is in all of it, more of me is committed in some areas than others; but me none the less.

A part of some of the things I like to do to gain new knowledge, which also defines me, is watch documentaries, preview or surf my favorite TV channels to extract different information. On the Science channel, one of the things the program creators like to do is propose a question or questions, and then let scientist attempt to answer the question scientifically as the show progresses. These scientist use different methods to answer these questions, whether it be with, theoretical physics, quantum physics, astrobiology, or astronomy. Most of the attempted answers are produced in theoretical form. In some cases, the scientists even try to present their theory as proven fact. But when you read the disclaimer at the bottom of the TV screen, you read that it is a scientific theory or the scientist use words such as may, could, or possible to explain the cause and effect of their theory.

Their scientific theory is a form of the freedom of speech privileges here in the USA, and a different way of looking at things. But there is a danger in looking at certain things too different, because there are those who would try to use the new found knowledge to capitalize on and confuse people about their life, their religious beliefs and faith concepts, and their moral obligations toward other humans. And the favorite questions the program producers love to propose most, "Is there a God?" in various different forms and how the question relate to the different problems that face humanity.

Ask almost any adult in the world what they believe is wrong with our world, you are sure to hear a litany of responses of real and perceived problems, ranging from international terrorism, disrespectful children, world hunger or lower wages. However, if you asked them what can they do about the problems he or she identifies, you very well may receive a response that can be summed up as, "What can I do? The problem is so big, and I'm not in any position to influence it." In my estimation the main problem today and throughout history is the human use and abuse of religion, how humans apply their religious beliefs, is their religion based on moral values of right and righteousness, or is it a construct of what is right to that individual; because religions can be produced from anything deemed valuable to the individual or a systematic philosophy to produce a level of comfort for the individual to repel external threats to the point where they employ others to except their philosophy.

Many people worry more about external threats, but often internal ones can make us the most vulnerable. God is looking for individuals today who will step up to serve Him; individuals who see beyond the need of the source of the problem and the possibility of solving it. Stepping up to serve the Lord often requires patience, preparation and perseverance. When we learn to prepare for God's service, we've taken a big step! And preparation for life is the key to our survival. In the eternal scope of our internal self, it is within my understanding of what God wants for us is to treat one another morally right governed by His righteous values and principles, which were intended as a way of life. The Lord God has expressed an eternal presence to the different races throughout historical time showing us how to apply the personalities of the God-self, but only one God.

There is a concept of one God who exists as three Personalities, which is the foundational platform for the Christian faith. The doctrine is vital for understanding who God is, how He relates to us, and how we are to relate to Him. The Trinity also raises many questions: How can God be both one and three? It is my belief that these are the three personal attributes of the God-self intermingle with humanity through time. If Jesus is God, why did He pray to God? Some of the people pondering such questions are Christians themselves who honestly struggle to understand or to articulate the mystery of God's triune nature. In admitting their struggle, today's Christians can be sure they're not the first to do so. Christians since at least the second century A.D. have made profound efforts to describe God's true nature so that all people not only come to know God, but to know Him as He is, but it is not right to impose our own personal beliefs on others to satisfy our personal egos as God's personified will. The Lord God does not need our unrighteous input as a holy conversion of help to solidify His presence here on Earth. So with all that being said, purposely written, this is not a book of conversion but one of enlightened conversation derived of a series of reflection papers, so I ask the question: **Does Morality Depend on Religion?**

1

"Nothing is beyond the power of God to act and perform, and what God does is in conformity with his own nature and will."

The Baker Illustrated Bible Dictionary

Just who are we connected to in this world?

After the Twin Towers fell, a journalist interviewed a woman on the streets of New York City and asked her if she was praying for the victims of the Trade Towers tragedy. The woman's reply was, "Pray to who, God caused the tragedy." Human beings blame a lot of things on God. As a whole, we don't truly follow the Holy Word of God, nor do we conform to the Omnipotent God.

In my estimation our generation is losing an awareness of the almighty God. God's answers for the past are still applicable for today. It seems as though we do not truly believe that God has a firm grip on all the world affairs. The difference is the creature's connection to the Creator, versus the creature's connection to its own creation.

The Almighty does not want to prevent humanity from creating on our own accord, but the Omniscient of God reserves the right to guide our thoughts on the use of our creations.

A Creature's Own Creation

When it comes to seeking for answers for our world as a whole, we have created a vastly different approach from that of our ancestors. Modern humans often rely only on intellect to solve problems without consulting God through prayer and meditation. It is only after we decide on a solution and our problem becomes worse, that we then seek a higher authority. Self-centered solutions keep appearing to put the world into a tailspin. The solution to end World War II with the atomic bomb polluted our planet. Then a bigger and more powerful hydrogen bomb was created, in attempt by one nation to gain an advantage over another. Our solution without consulting the all-knowing God creates problems for us, like what to do with radioactive waste from all those bombs. Not all of the creations of humanity are bad, but the wisdom we possess in the use of our creations, while with good intentions most often than not, create a new problem for humankind. We cannot perceive all of the future problems in the use of a creation, because humans think independent of one another. God has given humankind great moral beliefs to help guide us, all we have to do is apply them.

The Almighty does not want to prevent humanity from creating on our own accord, but the Omniscient of God reserves the right to guide our thoughts on the use of our creations. We are genetic creations of an Omnipotent Holy thought, designed to be a natural extension of a supernatural presence on earth, in the flesh. Human beings can do things that no other animal can do on earth. We can think, we can create, and we can make manifestations of our own thought, but we lack holy wisdom in daily application. Humankind has a tendency to destroy more than we create, and we even destroy when we put our creation into production. Perhaps one day, man will understand that an all-powerful God is at the core of everything upon this earth. Harmony with the *Omniscient* of God fills the vacuum of the many deficiencies of our limited wisdom. Is define in the Bake Bible Dictionary: "The English word derives from the Latin omnis ("all") and sciens ("knowing"). Though is not found in Scripture, the term accurately describes an exclusively divine attribute. God has perfect infinite knowledge of himself and everything actual and possible (1 Sam.23:8-13; Job 37:16;

Ps.33:13-15; 139:2-6; 147:5; Prov. 15:3; Isa. 40:14; 46:10; Dan. 2:22; Matt. 11:21-23; John 21:17; Acts 15:18; 1 Cor.2:10-11; Heb. 4:13; 1 John 3:20) God's omniscience is eternal, encompassing all things past, present, and future. It includes complete knowledge of all human choices, the occurrence of all events, and the outworking of all contingencies." (Longman III 2013).

What direction will we take?

One might ask, "What does it means to be omniscient?" It is the ability of knowing all things from beginning to end, with the gift of grace for support. The Almighty sees all and knows all, but He also controls all. With that thought in mind, through grace any outcome can be changed by the will of God. We may go in a direction that seems right to us, but is actually deadly or disastrous. Then something occurs which causes a different decision to be made. We did not see the original design for the previous disastrous direction, but we know the outcome of the present decision.

The example given could happen in reverse also, but the fact is God did not force the decision, or any other decision, because we are free thinking beings. There are times when the God Almighty uses strong measures of persuasion to prevent certain outcomes in human affairs. What is meant by strong measures of persuasion is this; a stronger more powerful thought or decision is used to counter another. But when evil tries to totally over take that which is good in human affairs, the Creator will allow some things to happen to keep the outcome in harmony for a more balanced solution, we call them natural disasters. God will never allow evil to totally overpower good in the world and these natural disasters causes us to think how we treat each other. A natural delicate balance is maintained, that keeps everything in harmony with one another, for the ultimate plan of the Creator.

Everything in harmony

The Omnipresence of God makes the universal harmony of all things possible. Regardless of what we believe, there is a presence in all things at the same time. Look at the rules or patterns of all things on our planet. We all have a DNA and molecular code that we know was created, but don't really understand how. Spiritual thinkers will understand that God is the source, and secular thinkers see dark matter, or some other scientific object as the source. The reason secular humans deny an all knowing presence is because we are free thinkers, and free thinkers who choose not to know the omniscient God, will believe they are in total control of their life. No one can totally control his or her own life. The idea of total control of one's life is a deception perpetrated by the evil one, which is the devil, to separate the creature from the Creator. When any human is completely separated from an all provision God, all types of mishaps are possible.

When mishaps occur in life, humans tend to count these occurrences as natural life occurrences. We feel our solutions can solve anything. Most human beings do not want to acknowledge the existence of a more holy and benevolent way of handling life's problems. God can deal with many things at once, with the right solution, and without deferment to humankind. The problem is not the Creator's solution, but the willingness of the creature to accept, and use the Creator's solution. As free thinkers, human beings seem to accept the most complicated solution to a problem that gives the most self-gratification and power. Even the religions of the world have adopted this complicated philosophy into their institutions. This complication is injected, by people taking control of these institutions through the years, and no religion is exempt in today's society. I am sad to admit that even in Christendom; some are starting to follow this dangerous and slippery slope.

Complexity does not make it right!

Historically, complex religions were developed when humans were used in carrying the foundation of Holy thought to all the different peoples of the world. Grateful receivers of this Holy thought, took the carriers' names or an important doctoral word for references, and created complex religious entities around the globe, completely different from what the Almighty intended. We have turned the Holy Word of God into plots and subplots of our own interpretation. World religions have let the philosophies of the secular world, the patriotism of countries, and the greed of unholy people take control of spiritual thought. The complexities in human thought are at the root of our most perplexing problems, and simplicity should be the order of the day.

We live in a world that does not fully comprehend the wisdom and knowledge of God. Man follows his own heart and has annihilated the direction of the righteous, and used the Holy words of God to fulfill lustful desires. History shows how different religions have gone on conquests in the name of spreading their version of the Omnipotent Holy Word. After a geographic area has been transformed into whatever religion is the majority, then commerce and knowledge flourishes. It's then that the children of greed and power take over to make everything complicated for their own benefit.

How can a finite being with so much carnal thinking, understand the eternal existence of God? Hallowed wisdom is better than logic. To begin to understand the eternal existence of God is to truly understand the mischievous inputs of a finite, coexistent thought, upon the pure word of God by humans.

Mankind has interfered with the thoughts and learning process of ourselves for selfish reasons, and made the pure word of God confusingly complicated throughout the world.

According to the Holy Bible, God's ways are not our ways, and God's wisdom surpasses our wisdom. With this being spiritual fact, we need to turn loose the carnal, finite mind, and embrace the spiritual mind of eternity, believe in the eternal being, and the growth of the eternal for all. The global benefit for everyone is righteous consciousness and a good beginning. If we humans could put aside our religious differences and embrace the religious commonality, and how they work together for the betterment of all humankind, we could truly walk in respect of one another. Think about the possibilities for the world without differences.

What a difference a phrase will make?

There is a phrase said by some which says: "For God I will live and for God I will die." For God I will live is the right approach, since the eternal one created the entire universe and caused the interdependence of all creation. Humankind must learn to live within the boundaries of this coexistence of interdependence in all creation. The Holy word of God teaches coexistence and some of the ancient principles for life of many religions, there is a commonality of coexistence written. We must not focus on the occult or barbaric religious practices, to base our arguments against other religions that teach righteousness, to make our own religion superior to another religion. Spiritual division continues to be the norm. My goal is not to put my belief above another, but show how the devil has put the major world religions against each other. Not good against evil, but righteous thinking against righteousness.

Somehow we must understand that there is a God who has Omnipresence. The eternal words and wisdom have been written and carried throughout our world. The problem has not been with, "for God I will live", but "for God I will die" part of the phrase. Humans have the silly notion that if we put our lives on the line, that God will be pleased with our dedication to the Eternal. The thought of putting our lives on the line for God is a reality we shouldn't have to encounter. We may ask our self: *Why would holiness and good, have you kill yourself or countless others to prove something?* Our patient Creator continues to withstand our ignorance. So let us concentrate on living a Righteous life and put aside finding ways to kill ourselves in an attempt to create a righteous cause. We owe God, ourselves, and the world, at least that much.

2

YOUR GOD AND THE INTERNAL YOU!

"Our inner self or soul is where we receive long lasting joys and pains of our existence."

Rev R. H. Moore, 1999

What have we done?

Throughout history, the struggles of humanity have been well documented. We can read in many different history books from various countries, and see how devastating humanity's struggles have been. Humanity has made gods and religions out of just about everything under the sun. Since the beginning of recorded history, humans have made gods out of wood, stones, and metal. We have used the description of birds, fish, and other animals as the source and power of events that happen in our world. Even in today's society, we still use the same materials for our little gods. But unlike the god statuary of the past, the statuesque are now computers, space shuttles, planetary observations, and massive weapons of destruction to define our existence. We have made new religions out of our modern thoughts and business practices, modern humans as a whole, put all their faith and belief in today's society; we worship this time period.

We have even gone as far as making gods out of pastors, preachers and religious teachers. We do this by naming our worship centers after them, seeking their approval and advise on everything we do. Among all the confusion of extensively seeking and putting blind faith in unstable practices of others advise, of Wall Street, the Omnipotent one is still there and remains the same as always, a stable presence within the holy written word and a guiding light for all, God's Holy Spirit.

Place your faith in the right source.
It's disturbing that many people have come to a junction in their lives that earthly things or another human being can replace God as the center of their life. Worldly possessions are limited in satisfaction, and people are limited on what they can do to help or satisfy another person. Putting intense faith in other people or worldly things creates a formula for failure and disappointment. We set ourselves up for failure and disappointment by

placing ourselves, people we know, leaders both secular and religious, on a pedestal. We must not go overboard with our affection and worship man, which ultimately belongs solely to God.

There are many who will not make a decision without consulting first with their bishop, pastor or pope, or religious figure head. This type of action is evident in most every religion around the world. Our religious leaders cannot be everywhere at the same time or know everything for everybody. They are merely humans with God given spiritual gifts and knowledge, and who also are prone to mistakes. I can say this because I am a preacher of the Gospel.

Some of our spiritual leaders have gifts and talents that cause others to view them with great reverence. These preachers, teachers, and pastors have a great ability to expound on the word of God with tremendous edification and exhilaration, which bring jubilation to others. The joy that comes from the preaching or teaching is highly appreciated by the church body; hence congregation members naturally want to show their gratitude to the deliverer of the teaching.

When we over zealously show affection of gratitude to any person, this borders on worshipping the person that is being honored. We may not intentionally want to worship others, but the obsessive affection can develop over a period of months, even years. If we do not stay mindful that God is the purpose of worship, then the worshipping of other humans or things will eventually happen.

There is a subtlety in human worship.

Once there was a minister's conference I attended. This was a minister's breakfast conference with a large number of preachers and pastors in attendance. The host pastor came in, and was placed at a table totally separate from all the other ministers. His food was brought to him on a silver plate with a cover made of silver and orange juice in a silver chalice, while everyone else used plastic cups and plates. After the food was placed in front of the host pastor, the person stood in front of the pastor until he gave the OK to leave! I am not sure if the person that brought in the food was instructed to wait to see if anything else was needed or not, but the entire scene appeared to boarder the line of worshipping another person. All of the other pastors and preachers should have been treated the same way.

The subtle worship of a leader is apparent in the religious sector. Every true believer of God must be made mindful of what is called hero worship in the secular sector. Let us not think for one moment that church goers are the only ones who tend to worship others unknowingly, or give heavy affection to. The secular world worships their favorite movie stars, sports heroes, music stars, business heroes and politicians, and even their own loved ones. The worship of others is very real, and as spiritual creatures, we have a tendency to worship whatever raises the spiritual levels of our inner self. The almighty God should always be the focal point of our worship.

The ancient people and civilizations recognized the almighty presence of a Higher Being in all things, but their expressions of this knowledge lead to idol and nature worship.

What about our inner self?

Our inner self or soul is where we receive long lasting joys and pains of our existence. In Genesis 1:26 & 27, of the Holy Bible, God created us in the likeness and image of Him. In chapter 2:7 of Genesis, He breathed into our human shells the breath of life to become living souls. Life is the breath of God. Author Huston Smith, in his book *World's Religions*, says the ancient Chinese call breath Ch'i, which literally means vital energy, or life force, a spirit. Since we are created in the image and likeness of God, the soul of man will forever be in want of a being higher than himself. We are spirit beings residing in the flesh, but have an avenue to God if we so choose. When we truly worship the Creator, we give credence to the original relationship of God's presence in the human soul.

In any relationship, when closely related love comes together, only joy can abide in that relationship. It is in the best interest of humans to worship the one from which we came. To worship anyone, or anything else, is a worship of idols or self and not the creator. The created, man in this case, should never worship another creature or creation, because we can never give each other eternal joy or life according to the holy scripture of God. Man made things will only give us temporal joy. Human worship will inevitably bring disappointments, because of our frailties.

We are so limited in everything that we do when it comes to eternity of life and liberty. All humans have the internal drive for self-preservation and most of our decisions will be based on self. Without the guidance of the Holy Spirit of God, our effort at self-preservation will fully dominate our total being and thinking. If we become totally selfish in our thinking and actions, we will limit our worth to other human beings.

Humans tend to rely on others on how to live life. Why would we give so much acknowledgment to another human who has flaws? We should rely on The Holy Word of God on how to live life and in our worship. Hopefully, we can stop worshipping our leaders and heroes. Some people will call the relationship of hero worshipping, giving respect. Some people will say that giving accolades are just human nature, but the Holy Bible shows us that it is idol worshipping, because when you give another person the majority of the credit or accolades for your success that is worship of an idol being. Idol worshipping is in conflict with God and against His commandments. Even the greatest one to walk this earth, in my opinion, points us toward the Omnipotent Hallowed God and that person is none other than Jesus the Christ.

The ancient people and civilizations recognized the almighty presence of a Higher Being in all things, but their expressions of this knowledge lead to idol and nature worship. The worship of nature is based on the personification of natural phenomena. The people of ancient times personified various objects and forces of nature and worshipped them as gods. "In these nature-worships," the late Edward Carpenter, the author of *Pagan and Christian Creeds*, writes:

There may be discerned three fairly independent streams of religious or quasi-religious enthusiasms: (1) that connected with the phenomena of the heavens; the movements of the sun, planets, and stars, and the awe and wonderment they excited; (2) that connected with the seasons and the very important matter of the growth of vegetation and food on the earth: and (3) that connected with mysteries of sex and reproduction. It is obvious that these three streams would mingle and inter fuse with each other a good deal; but as far as they were separable, the first would tend to create solar heroes and sun-myths; the second, vegetation-gods and personifications of nature and the earth-life; while the third would throw its glamour over the other two, and contribute to the projection of deities of demons worshipped with all sorts of sexual and phallic rites. (pp. 19-20)

With the worship of nature, ancient people misunderstood the revelation of God's presence in nature and within themselves. These ancient people made gods from the things in nature: sky gods, fertility gods, gods for the moon, the sun, animals, etc.

There have been, evidence of these different nature gods through numerous civilizations, traced to the earliest dates of Egypt. Noted author John G. Jackson, of the book *Man, God, and Civilization*, writes:

> Among the ancient Egyptians, the earth was personified as a male deity by the name of Seb, Keb, or Geb, and his consort was the sky-goddess Nut. In Egyptian art, Seb is shown in human form and with his head adorned with a crown or a goose... The earth was to be the body of Seb as well as his house; for the earth was called the House of Seb, just as the underworld was called the House of Osiris, and the air, the House of Shu. Strange to say, on one occasion, Seb laid an egg; and this egg, in due time, burst asunder and gave birth to the sun-god, in the form of a mysterious bird known as the

> Phoenix… Seb was quite properly called the Father of the Gods, for the following divinities were his children: Osiris, Set, Horus the Elder, Isis, and Nephthys. The Greek mythologists identified Seb with their own Cronus; for as Osiris was said to have mutilated his father Seb, likewise Cronus is said to have mutilated his father Uranus. (pp. 83-84)

As there is evidence in the Greek writings about the different earth and nature gods, there is also evidence from Indians of Peru, ancient Sumerians, Mexicans, Babylonians, the Chaldees, and many other ancient peoples of the world. All have some roots traceable to the worship of nature and the earth. An absence of God's spirit equals an idol who will take God's place.

A barbarian sacrifice does not please God!

We have learned from ancient history, that some civilizations made human and animal sacrifices to various gods. *"The occurrence of human sacrifice appears to have been widespread and its intentions various, ranging from communion with a god and participation in his divine life to expiation and the promotion of the earth's fertility… (Britannica, 1987, 26:840:1a)"* Some of these acts were recorded in the Holy Bible, 2nd Kings 3:27 says: *"Then he took his eldest son that should have reigned in his stead, and offered him for a burnt offering upon the wall. And there was great indignation against Israel: and they departed from him, and returned to their own land."* The sacrifice was performed because the king of Moab, whom Israel was friends with, wanted to win a big battle. Also recorded in Jeremiah 19:5: *"They have built also the high places of Baal, to burn their sons with fire for burnt offerings unto Baal, which I commanded not, nor spake it, neither came it into my mind: Therefore, behold, the days come, saith the Lord, that this place shall no more be called Tophet, nor The Valley of the son of Hinnon, but The Valley of slaughter."*

The Britannica (1987) also states that in many societies human victims gave place to animal substitutes or to effigies made of dough wood, or other materials. Thus moving away from violet offering, but there are a few occultist cultures still trying to hold on to the sacrificial practices today by imposing a modern martyrdom tradition on many people. This human sacrificial practice is a barbaric way to please their god and as a personal observation, my belief is, a martyr is someone who chooses to stand up for right and righteousness, then lose their life in the process, not as a tactical means imposed on a group of people for political gain.

So people are doing and have done many things to please their god, but a lot of the things people have done are not required by God. Think about those who would strap a bomb to themselves, or use some other devise to commit senseless acts of terrorism to others, in the name of their god, with the idea of pleasing God for a better life in Heaven. Even the historical religious wars and conquest of Christians and Muslims, and others alike, all believe to be doing God's bidding. Why do most humans think engaging in war and conquests helps in doing the bidding of God, in spreading the Omniscient of God?

Because the revelation of God is evident in all of creation, many humans have misinterpreted the essence of God's being, words, and actions toward us. This has led to many wars, hardships, and religions. I believe God wants humankind to understand God's nature in the environment and the universe. The life force of God is in all things of nature. In the Holy Bible, Genesis 1:1-2 says: *"In the beginning God created the heaven and the earth. And the earth was without form, and void; and darkness was upon the face of the deep. And the Spirit of God moved upon the face of the waters."*

The Spirit is God's life force, which is evident in all of creation including us.

God's spirit makes all things interdependent.

The life force, or Spirit of God identifies all things in the supernatural and all things are linked together in the natural also. According to the Bible, Genesis 2:7; *"And the Lord God formed man of the dust of the ground, and breathed into his nostrils the breath of life; and man became a living soul."* Not only was the breath of life breathed into man and the spirit of God upon the earth, but man was formed by the use of the same type of matter building blocks, from the earth, which unifies humankind with the rest of creation. The ancient Chinese recognized this fact in the Taoist tradition, they believed in the Ch'i. According to Huston Smith, in his book *World's Religions,* "Ch'i was maximized with three things: matter, movement, and their minds." (pp.130)

The life force, or Spirit of God identifies all things in the supernatural and all things are linked together in the natural also.

God's spirit or breath makes all things interdependent upon each other. This was revealed to the ancient civilizations of the world, but they chose to worship God's presence in all of creation as individual gods. The Creator wanted humankind to see the divine in all of nature, and in ourselves; and also to respect humankind and nature. This is evident in the notion that if humankind would revere the highest and *only* authority, God, then humans would respect themselves and nature, since the Spirit of God is shown in all things. If only we would slow down long enough to see, hear, and enjoy the Spirit of God in the world, maybe we can save ourselves and also our planet. Kathleen Fischer, in her book, *Reclaiming the Connection A Contemporary Spirituality, says:*

> "Like body and spirit, history and nature
> have also been separated from one an-
> other. Human events have assumed cen-
> ter stage, though played out against the
> backdrop of nature. This is a distorted
> picture of reality; nature and human his-
> tory are themselves intertwined." (pp.40)

For the most part, humans have chosen not to see the divine existence in nature, or in us. If we did, we would not destroy this beautiful world of ours or countless other inhabitants of the planet for ill gain. Because so many people have not really applied the life giving disciplines of the almighty God in any religion. History has proven that we love to focus on the differences of the religions and any destructive thing which would make one superior to another. What we have not realized is there is a supreme being that has given us disciplines and principles to live by, to maximize life in this world.

Let us have a revival!

For a better world, we must comprehend the revivalistic knowledge the Creator has given us. What is revivalistic knowledge you may ask? *It is an extension of the word revivalist meaning; a meeting led by an evangelist to stir up religious feeling: both words are by products of the word revival meaning a reviving or being revived; to bring or coming back into use; restoration to vigor or activity. (Webster's New World*

Dictionary, pp. 512) Humans need to be restored to a deepness of love and respect for each other. We need to understand that the ways of God, have been shown and given to us down through the centuries. If humanity is to survive, there needs to be understanding of the ways of God.

To be revived into the knowledge of God, is to understand that there is a higher being or consciousness, who has given us knowledge of certain truths to live by. These truths allow humans to free themselves unto life and liberate themselves from death. In the Holy Bible, Romans 6: 22 & 23 states: *"But now being made free from sin, and become servants to God, ye have your fruit unto holiness, and the end everlasting life. For the wages of sin is death; but the gift of God is eternal life through Jesus Christ our Lord."* The sin in a person's life blocks them from the knowledge of God, which causes them to die spiritually. This death will not allow the individual to properly know themselves. Sin blocks the spiritual link between our inner self or soul and God the eternal spirit.

As a person continues to seek only the pleasures of life, these pleasures go on to widen the gap between a person's true self, and the eternal presence of God. What happens is the person feeds on things which satisfy the ego, and anything that is fed will grow. So the ego grows, which causes an individual to think he or she is the sole purpose of living and nothing else matters. What the person fails to realize is that no person has created themselves. Thomas Merton, the author of *The Silent Life*, wrote: *"…although God our Father made us free, he did not make us omnipotent.*

We are capable of becoming perfectly godlike, in all truth, by freely receiving from God the gift of his light, and his love, and his freedom in Christ, the incarnate Logos. But in so far as we are implicitly convinced that we ought to be omnipotent of ourselves we usurp to ourselves a god likeness that is not ours… In our desire to be "as gods"-a lasting deformity impressed in our nature by original sin---we seek that one might call a relative omnipotence: the power to have everything we want, to enjoy everything we desire, to demand that all our wishes be satisfied and that our will should never be frustrated or opposed. It is the needs to have everyone else bow to our judgment and accept our declarations as law. It is the insatiable thirst for recognition of the excellence we so desperately need to find in ourselves to avoid despair. This claim to omnipotence, our deepest secret and our inmost shame, is in fact the source of all our sorrows, all our unhappiness, all our dissatisfactions, all our mistakes and deceptions. It is a radical falsity…" (pp. 14-15).

If humankind truly wants to evolve, we as planetary neighbors need to genuinely understand that there is an all wise being, holy and sanctified unto all wisdom, knowledge, and understanding. Through the major religions of the world, God has provided the very essence of the God self. When the text of these religions and not the occult, are placed together to read as one, then we can understand clearly the way to higher consciousness that the Creator intended us to have. Every race of people in the world has their own cultures, beliefs, and understanding of things. God has addressed each race for the betterment of all kind. Since everything in the universe is interconnected, God's mannerism is the best for all of life period. The sooner we learn this truth, the quicker all the people of the world can live fully, and put aside our petty, personal differences.

3

THE PERSONAL EFFECT

"For in this behest I saw a marvelous compassion that our Lord hath in us for our woe, and a courteous promising of clear deliverance."

Julian of Norwich

Can contemporary life effect holy relationships?

In today's society we live a better way of life, materialistically, than our fathers and mothers who lived before us in a lot of different ways. But we have lost some quality personal and interment relationships in the process.

Men and women are in the workforce, we have commercial daycare, instant dinners and are very fast paced and quick to change. The majority of the time we think a fast paced lifestyle and quick change is best.

So many people have adapted to this method of living by trying to please themselves only and show compassion to others when it is beneficial to them. There are those who adopted this fast pace lifestyle and have tried to impose this thought on the church. In a few cases this philosophy has become as a religion, like the extreme emphasis placed on the computer revolution and the internet phenomenon. How can we continue this modern fast pace lifestyle and be happy based off the ungodly long hours so many spend on these devices? We crave the instant information computer technology brings and the instant wealth by E-trade with good or bad intentions.

If we look closer at the modern lifestyle, some people who have great influence are trying to influence the church. The elitist church attendant tries to take advantage of his or her influence and wealth, to make changes in the modern church. The changes may be beneficial to the church building but the principles of God, which benefit the universal church, become jeopardized. Their demands are very subtle, and if it were possible they would probably impose that God should change too. We know God never changes, but the church consists of individuals who do change from time to time. We change to make ourselves happy, and to be more stable in our lives, but we do not know how to truly understand ourselves as purposed by Julian of Norwich.

What is the Julian experience to
personally knowing God?

Author Julian of Norwich expresses in the book, *Revelations of Divine Love*, that humans are unhappy, incomplete, and sinful creatures without the love of God. She explains through personal experiences of some pain, suffering and sickness in her life, how she came to know God's compassion, love and personality. One may ask, how can we know God personally and why would anyone want to know God through sickness? Julian answers the question with purity of thought, by first understanding that only God can truly help her understand why. She thought that it is not necessary to comprehend everything about life in this world, or to establish a personal thinking with God. Julian explains that compassion of God, the passion of Jesus, and the revealing of the Holy Ghost, is the mind of God. Out of the Trinity of God, all humans can be fulfilled in this life by receiving the love, joy, peace of mind, compassion, devotion, dedication, drive, energy, respect and tolerance of other people that come to our mind from God. She lets the reader know that by her personal experiences, the understanding of God's being becomes the essence of knowing.

Julian had hands on awareness of Christ's passion through sickness, pain and suffering. It is not that she wanted pain constantly or even a painful death by her sickness. Julian believes that only through a degree of pain and suffering will the creature know what the creator demonstrated on the cross to pull us back to God sinless. A fleshly or sinful thought, must be crucified to obtain a sinless or Godly thought, which comes through the Christ our redeemer. No one wants to die or take the pain that comes with it, but a life without God is not worth living. Listen to the voice of Julian as she writes:

> "It is more blissful that man be taken from pain, than pain is taken from man; for if pain be taken from us it may come again: therefore it is a sovereign comfort and blissful beholding in a loving soul that we shall be taken from pain. For in this behest I saw a marvelous compassion that our Lord hath in us for our woe, and a courteous promising of clear deliverance." (49)

Julian learned during her sickness that God became personal with her by healing her and taking her through the pain that was personal to her. When pain and suffering hits us so hard we only seek deliverance, and we really do not care who delivers us. Most of the time if the pain and suffering is life threatening we become personal, or close to those around us. We can also identify with those who have gone through similar circumstances and those who have helped us.

Is there a personal touch to life?

Humans also like a personal touch to their daily lives. For example, the personal touch of a dressmaker, or a tailor, the lifestyle, or clothing we choose, or even the achievements of our leaders we can identify with. God knows our way of thinking too and has worked personally in human affairs. But humankind as a whole has missed the mark to be personally touched by the presence of God, or the mind of God, by not spiritually embracing the Holy Scripture and using intellectual reasoning only.

God has been revealing His purpose to humankind throughout the centuries, to reconcile us back to our original state of a spiritual being.

Many people perceive the eternal one as both distant, and not personal, so we continue to rely on our abilities and knowledge. Relying on our self-knowledge has caused us to position ourselves to the edge of self-annihilation, but the compassionate God of salvation will extend the existence of humanity, since God is the common source for all. The idea of a savior is much needed for humans, because a savior makes God both personal, and human. This idea of a savior god is widespread and ancient. Author John G. Jackson in his book, *Man, God, and Civilization*, writes:

The New Testament of the Christian Bible contains the alleged biography of a virgin-born savior of the human race. The Christians, in this case, as in many others, were anticipated by the pagans; for virgin born gods who sacrificed themselves for the good of the race were quite common in the myths and legends of the heathen nations of antiquity. The Reverend Charles H. Vail, in a scholarly study, *The World's Saviors,* records the stories of miraculous births of fifteen other saviors, who lived before the Christian era. The names of these world's saviors are Krishna of India, Gautama of India, Horus of Egypt, Tammuz of Babylonia, Mithra of Persia, Zoroaster of Persia, Quetzalcoatl of Mexico, Bacab of Yucatan, Huetzilopochtli of Mexico, Freyr of Scandinavia, Attis of Phrygia, Bacchus of Greece, Adonis of Syria, Yu of China, Jesus. (pp.123)

There are a number of these so called savior gods, but only one person really taken seriously, even our method of date keeping state the fact with (AD), after death of Jesus the Christ. So many savior gods may cause a person to ask, why are there so many of these types of gods through human history? God has been revealing His purpose to humankind throughout the centuries, to reconcile us back to our original state of a spiritual being. The Omnipotent one has been trying to get our attention for many centuries. He wants to be more personal to us, but our knowledge has severely crippled our understanding of an Omnipotent God. And we have tried to explain a holy existence by our different cultural names for the Godly common source.

The cultural names for these ancient savior gods seem to come from a common source passed through human history, and the source for most seems to have come from Egypt. Author Jocelyn Rhys has an instructive discourse on this:

> Horus was said to be the parthenogenetic child of the Virgin Mother Isis. In the catacombs of Rome,…. statues of this Egyptian divine Mother and Infant still survive from the early Christian worship of the Virgin and Child to which they were converted…Statues of the goddess Isis with the child Horus in her arms were common in Egypt, and were exported to all neighboring and remote countries, where they are still to be found with new names attached to them; Christian in Europe, Buddhist in Turkestan, Taoist in China and Japan. Figures of the Virgin Isis, does duty as representation of Mary, of Hariti, of Kuan-Yin, of Kwannon, and of other Virgin Mothers of gods. (pp. 115-16)

Generally humans have a problem with a god that cannot feel the pains of a human, emotion of a human, or personality of a human; some people have a problem with a supernatural savior that identifies with human creation. Nature already identifies with eternity by simple existence. The universe has been around much longer than human beings, but the question is, how was Jesus Christ the Savior God and human simultaneously, creating a paradox. The reality of it all is that with God all things are possible and nothing is impossible for the Creator. Think for a moment about the conception of a child. All females carry the egg or seed of the human body. The males carry the life force which is injected into the seed, by the coming together of male and female, to start the life of a human being. Through the breakthroughs of science, this solely natural process for many years can now be performed without human physical interaction.

The God-Man or Savior knows all the ways and attributes of the divine, and can feel all the pains, desires, and emotions of a human being. Now God is personal with humans.

Was there a need of a human mother?
In the past when a male and female could not produce a child, they had to adopt a child, or one of the partners had to go unto someone else, to produce a child.

Infertility is no longer a stumbling block in child reproduction in our society anymore. Couples with fertility problems can now use fertility enhancing drugs, or artificial insemination. According to Crooks & Baur (2014), artificial insemination is a means whereby a woman can achieve pregnancy not involving sexual intercourse. There are a number of reasons why a woman would choose artificial means to achieve pregnancy. For example, a woman's immune system may be reject her partner's sperm as invading molecules, she may have issues with the cervix, such as cervical scarring, cervical blockage from endometriosis, or other reasons.

There are also different techniques of artificial insemination, the most commonly used method is IUI (Intrauterine Insemination), or if the women is unable to go to term for whatever the reason, there is IVF (In Vitro Fertilization) (Crooks & Baur, 2014). IVF is the process of fertilization by manually combining an egg and sperm in a laboratory dish and the process is combined with a procedure known as embryo transfer, which involves physically placing the embryo in the uterus of a surrogate mother.

The most typical cases of surrogate motherhood are those in which the surrogate is artificially inseminated with the husband's sperm because the wife of the couple desiring a child is infertile. By the mid-1980s doctors were able to implant an embryo created by in vitro fertilization in the womb of a surrogate, thus permitting an infertile couple to obtain a child who was *genetically their own. (*The New Encyclopedia Britannica, *11:pp. 413:3b)*

A person may ask what Jesus has to do with me. The Messiah was fully human. All the temptations of life could affect him, but Jesus remained holy and true to God. With the life of Christ, there is proof that a human can go through life and still be in direct communion with God.

If humans can reproduce our own kind through the miracles of modern scientific methods, and can genetically create an child apart from sexual relations, then what can prevent God from using a similar procedure (virginal conception, Longman III 2013), to produce a God- Man Savior? Since God knows the DNA code for life, no male sperm is needed for fertilization of the woman's seed. A virgin woman is used, in Bible terms means the womb and seed are holy. Now God's Holy Spirit is implanted into the holy seed of the woman, and the genetics of God and human become one. The divine one creates a being fully God, and fully human (a second Adam type), apart from sexual relations. St. John 1:14 of the Holy Bible records: *And the Word was made flesh, and dwelt among us, (and we beheld his glory, the glory as of the only begotten of the Father), full of grace and truth.*

The God-Man or Savior knows all the ways and attributes of the divine, and can feel all the pains, desires, and emotions of a human being. Now God is personal with humans. All the rules, religious disciplines, and social awareness, would apply to the very essence of divine presence. No longer can humankind point a finger at the Holy One and say, there is no compassion for humans by the divine, because to go through pains and sufferings that humans have gone through, will identify the Creator with the creature, and create a deep sense of commitment, and mercy for the human race. There is love and understanding for each individual because the divine has gone through the same or similar experiences, which seems to be so important to us.

Let's examine the well-documented Jesus, the Christ, as an example for a moment. As believers of God we know that we are governed by human laws and live by God's laws. Jesus had to walk among both set of laws and remain true to both. If we look deeper we will find that most of the human laws that govern daily human affairs for today derive from the ten commandments of the Bible. Jesus, did not violate any of the Ten Commandments, and thus did not violate any human laws. A Roman officer speaks on Jesus behalf in St. Luke 23:4: *Then said Pilate to the chief priests and to the people, I find no fault in this man.*

What does a savior have to do with me?

A person may ask what Jesus has to do with me. The Messiah was fully human. All the temptations of life could affect him, but Jesus remained holy and true to

God. With the life of Christ, there is proof that a human can go through life and still be in direct communion with God. Every person has a divine inner spirit within themselves if only we, like the Messiah, would allow the righteous principles of God to govern our lives. Our problem is we still continue to do things in humanly fashion, and deny the presence of an Omnipotent being. We do not accept the Savior that God gave us, but we continually accept the human version of a savior. Author Huston Smith, author of the book *World's Religions*, writes:

> To begin with, though the Christian announcement of a God-Man was as startling in its day as it is ours, the shock attaches to opposite poles. Because it is difficult to believe that a human being can be divine, we find the shocking feature of the Incarnation to be what is says about Jesus: that he was God. In its own world, however, the dividing line between the human and the divine was so faint emperors routinely claimed to be divine--that a struggling sect's claim that its founder was divine raised few eyebrows. What else is new? (pp.219)

Humanity just does not have the wisdom or moral sense to achieve unity for our world. History has shown us that beings such as ourselves simply do not have the wisdom to rule, or protect each other with righteousness and justice. With all our hatred, dishonest ways and prejudices, we still believe in other humans' ability to lead, guide, and save us from ourselves. We call them presidents, kings, magistrates, prime ministers, and emperors. All these people have consistently enslaved us, economically, politically, socially, and militarily, throughout history.

Humans, for some strange reason, have a desire to be ruled and governed by other humans, and most of the time we put great faith in their abilities. Yet God has given us a savior, Jesus the Christ, who was concerned about human lives, willing to assume the limitations of human life, willing to suffer on human behalf, and willing to be sacrificed to reconcile us back to God. All we have to do is believe that the sacrifice lived, died, and arose back to God, to unlock the inner self to holiness; it's like a spiritual key to the Omnipresence. God has allowed the death of Jesus to bring enlightenment and life to us all. Most humans would rather put their faith in the ones who have already enslaved them. We give ourselves far too much credit in human affairs, and the Eternal One not enough credit.

The world community must realize that humans are more than just physical beings. We are spiritual beings also, and each individual has a spirit all their own. This spirit or inner self is what make humans so unique. We can think for ourselves and explore our inner self, but we must take caution in the inner self exploration. Let us be careful not to base everything on our inner self-awareness only, because if we base everything on spiritual awareness of self only, we will feed the Spiritual ego, and portentously breed self-righteousness. There are times we must go beyond self to help our human Inner self. We help our self by being aware of and focus on the Eternal Spirit of God, which is beyond us, yet eternally present. Prayer and meditating on God are the keys to Godly awareness.

4

PRAYER AND SPIRITUAL GROWTH

"It comes when the soul is enjoying fellowship with God through the reading and meditation of His word and prayer."

Alfred P Gibbs

Do you really believe that there is power in prayer?

Since the beginning of recorded history, there has been a great quest for power, the power to rule, the power to make a difference in life, and the power to change the world. There have been many rulers like Rameses III, Nebuchadnezzar, Augustus Caesar, and Adolf Hitler, just to name a few, who for a brief period had a sense of power. History has clearly shown that their power quest was both futile and finite in scope. The real power is transcendent, boundless, and infinite. The most exciting thing about this kind of power is this, it can be distributed, it is very accessible, and most of all it is obtainable. The reason for believing in the distribution, the accessibility, and the obtainable power is because God is the source, and prayer is the power fuse. Prayer is a method of communication where a person can be in touch with themselves and with the Creator of all things. We can use prayer to empower ourselves and others as well, to make a difference in our personal lives, and to change the things that disturbs us most. Let us see how prayer can make the difference, to empower, and change personal lives.

A large percentage of people to today are in a state of disarray with problems on every side, and seemly to them, there are no answers. They get caught up in their own problems, and those problems overtake them and crush their spirit. That is the reason I like to use the philosophy, that it takes more energy to worry about a problem, than it does to solve it. The Omniscient is present and operating in our world and the proper thing to do is to ask God for a solution. In St. Matthew 7:7 of the Holy Bible we can read:

Ask, and it shall be given you; seek, and ye shall find; knock, and it shall be opened unto you. In this passage of scripture, Jesus lets us know that we should ask God first for what is needed. When we begin to go to the Eternal One in prayer, the focal point is no longer on the problem, but now on the solution giver anticipating the solution. This will allow your inner self or soul, to become connected to your spiritual mind and the infinite wisdom of God. Now you become a seeker who is willing to look for the answer from a more powerful source than yourself.

God, who is the more powerful source, can show you the different doorways to solutions. These doorways are presented to the recipient as options for him, or her to use, but the choices are the recipient's to make, even if the recipient chooses their own solution. When the recipient chooses solutions freely given by God, then they can stop using so much energy on the problem and give way to the solution. When you are one with God, the Holy Spirit can flow freely, and the door way that is right for you becomes very clear. That is why it is so important for each person to be one with the Creator. In the book, *Reclaiming the Connections, A Contemporary Spirituality*, author Kathleen Fischer expresses it this way;

> God is not only the source of order in our world, but also the source of newness. God knows all possibilities. One role of prayer is to open us to these new ways of looking at things. Judged from this viewpoint prayer should enable us to view the world in a fresh way, to see opportunities where we had not noticed them before... (25)

Some people of our so-called advanced society do not believe in God or prayer. They claim to live by real world thinking. Real world thinking is okay when things are going right for you, but there are times when there is so much going wrong in your world that you do not have the power to correct it and you feel powerless. When powerlessness overwhelms a person often times that is when they decide to seek a higher power or authority. Prayer is the connection, because this form of communication let's an individual seek places other than temporal methods. There was a time in my youth when the realness of prayer became apparent to me. At the young age of about six years old I wanted a puppy extremely bad, so I asked my father for one. He told me that I could not have a puppy because the puppy would grow up to be a dog. The answer given by my father was devastating to me, but an answer was available for me.

Sunday school was a big part of my life, and the lessons learned in Sunday school had a big impression on me. One of those lessons was that people could go to God in prayer and ask for what they wanted. So one night before I went to bed, my prayer was for a puppy. I believed that a puppy would be given to me because I asked God for the puppy. The prayer was not answered right away it took some months before my prayer came to pass. So one cool rainy day, my father brought home a small black and white puppy, it was not like the dogs of my friends, but I did not care because the puppy was mine.

The infusion of hope is a great faith builder.
The personal life experience just shared was the very first time that spiritual communication to God, through prayer, became real for me. I truly believed that a puppy would be received by me, so I didn't worry about a puppy, nor did I worry my parents. In the Christian community a childlike belief is called faith. In Hebrews 11:1 of the Holy Bible, faith is described in this fashion; *Now faith is the substance of things hoped for, the evidence of things not seen.* Faith is a spiritual event and we must grow in it.

Sometimes in this spiritual walk of life, the way to spiritual enlightenment and social fulfillment cannot be fully seen and the path is blocked. But hope is the mechanism for change, so we depend heavily upon hope and in the process patience is built. This in turn changes the individual who is seeking an answer and causes the individual to grow spiritually when the answer is received. Furthermore, other individuals who are in the divine will of the prayer can have a change of heart. This was the case of my father when the opportunity was presented to get that puppy for me.

There is a power within us if we surrender to holy thinking.
The power of prayer cannot only change our immediate world, but also the world around us. Everyday individuals in this world make decisions based upon solutions that confront them. We as individuals also

make decisions based upon an affirmation of our own individual prayer or someone else's. Author Kathleen Fischer writes:

> ...In the ongoing divine relationship to the world, God takes account of and receives our prayers. They are of course transformed in God's life, but they insert new love and strength into the situation of the person we are praying for, and they are received by God and become a real factor in God's ongoing guidance of the world. We have made a difference. Prayer not only changes us; it affects God and those we pray for. (pp.23)

There are masses of people who feel like they have no power to change things in their life, the life of their peers, or the world around them. There are several reasons why this type of hopelessness emerges. Maybe there is a sense of loneliness, when new possibilities are not visible. This loneliness overshadows the inner spirit, which produces a self-afflicting doubt and confusion, and when this happens, the person can feel that nothing can go right for them or anyone else. Sometimes a sense of hopelessness emerges when a person feels like the world is too vast to change, or to make a difference in someone else's life. This vast mode of thinking causes the individual to feel too small and insufficient, and too powerless to do anything. What these individuals do not realize is they have access to a vast and infinite source of power called the Spirit of God. By the supernatural spirit, the individual can become interconnected with the Omniscient God, and with the spirit of others, for whom we pray for or being prayed for by others, an individual can be empowered. This interconnected empowerment is worked through intercessory prayer.

Intercessory prayer can work wonders for any individual, by taking the focus off of oneself, and placing the focus of your spiritual mind to help someone else. This gives you a sense of oneness with another person, and bonds the two individuals together personally. The intercessory prayer becomes increasingly personal, when someone tells another of their situation and asks another person to pray for them, or the listener says they will pray for the individual. The spiritual empowerment by two personally coming together to strengthen one, helps both to commune with God. Fischer writes:

> In addition to making a difference to God, intercessory prayer is a means of strengthening human community. Our decisions create a different world for others to interact with. Since in a process view every entity is affected by every other entity in space time, sin poisons the

> whole cosmos, while love enriches that cosmos. Prayers of intercession are expressions of love in a faith context. The profound experience of prayer lives not only in the separate self; intercession is one of the ways of deepening communion with others as well as with God, thus bringing about the reign of God. (pp.24)

Another way to acquire empowerment for change is interactive prayer. This is the process of two or more individuals praying with each other, simultaneously. Interactive prayer can be done in the same room, over the phone, or at an appointed time in different places. Each person must be fully aware of the others praying, and praying about the same thing. The Holy Spirit of God connects with each person and searches the sincere heart, and then God honors the prayer based on the perfect will or path. We could connect different true believers of God around the world, by using interactive prayer and make a significant change of our world. This is an act of inclusion and not separatism, to build a united humanity for peace without dominating each other. Maybe just maybe, we could empower and inspire each other to use righteous living, to govern and direct all human affairs.

There have been many ways to bring different communities together to empower and to bring hope. The most moving, inspiring, and power enriching act is community prayer. The community coming together for prayer at a local church, or a group of individuals, who may or may not know each other, coming together in one place. There may or may not be a spiritual leader to direct the group in prayer communication. Each individual prays to the Eternal God simultaneously and on one accord. As the community prayer session continues, individual breakthroughs transpire and spiritual excitement fills the area, which allows each person to be important to the community and spiritual growth through corporate prayer is accomplished by all.

Prayer is an important and essential part to human spiritual growth, and well-being. Without prayer and meditation, it is almost impossible to obtain direct communication with the Omniscient and obtain Eternal Power. The more we pray, the more God has the opportunity to reveal the holy presence of the eternal spirit to us. In James 5:16, of the Holy Bible, it reads: *Confess your faults one to another, and pray one for another, that ye may be healed. The effectual fervent prayer of a righteous man availeth much.*

So what are you as a human being really looking for?
We as human beings are always wanting something, or looking for something to better ourselves or to gain an advantage, so we seek that which we want. If the thing we seek is out of our reach, and we know that it is out of

our reach, this is the perfect opportunity for the eternal Spirit or God to work in our lives. As the invisible is made visible, then there is spiritual growth. Growth happens because we know it within ourselves. The thing we sought was not obtained under our own power or knowledge. The more we pray or talk with God, the more spiritual power we receive, and the more powerful we feel, to make a difference in our world. This feeling of power comes because, as an individual prays, his or her spirit communes with God's spirit to become as one. The oneness with God and creation will enable the individual to not only see things as they are, but to be able to see things as they could be. So what humans are really looking for is to commune with the eternal. To know God spiritually, is when you really see God.

5

THE TRUE SELF

"Normally, personality development is based on the uniqueness of each individual. Sense of self develops from infancy. Interest is on the present and on what one is becoming. The approach has a future orientation and stresses self-awareness before action."

Existential therapy, Corey

My God, may I ask you a question?

Many people believe that the search for varying ways to reach spiritual truths is a never ending conquest for humans. For centuries people have wondered what is life's purpose and if there is more to life than what exists. This time period is no different than previous ones, and these questions appear on the surface, to never have been answered or have they? Many religions, both Eastern and Western, present compelling views on the question of more to life and human existence. Each religion feels their path is the correct path, all competing for the minds of people. Eastern religions such as Buddhism, Confucianism, Hinduism, and Taoism have developed an inner self philosophy to try to address the questions of the ages. This inner self philosophy expressed by eastern religions, coincide with a philosophy of my own, "I'm in competition with no one but myself". And as a Christian minister, there is an assurance of non-competition on my part that brings a level of comfort for want brings my inner peace. Oneness through Christ brings an inner peace to Christians which is vital to the Christian faith.

My philosophy of being in competition with no one else but yourself should cause an individual to want to make themselves a better person. To become a better person can come from different ways. It can be spiritual, social, or physical. For any given person, one, all, or any combination of these elements can be used to better oneself. Since you are competing with yourself, what others receive or gain, either materially or spiritually, will not affect your self-worth. You are not affected because your main focus is not on want other people have or what they achieve. If a person stays focused on the betterment of themselves, then it will help keep them from focusing on fleshly desires such as envy, jealousy, and hatred. That does not mean you cannot learn from others to better yourself. It is this thought process that has made the study of Eastern religions and traditions fascinating by many.

The Eastern Religions may seem absurd to some Westerners, or maybe confusing to others, but one thing is for sure, these forms of religions are both needed and necessary, because not everyone will embrace western religion. If others will embrace righteousness instead of evil, it can be beneficial to all. Think about it for a moment, there are vastly different people in the world, with different emotions and different cultures. Among different people and cultures, God has shown there is a cognizance of a higher being. The religions of the East and West convey the fact of an Omnipotent God, or spirit with similarities in their teachings. These similarities are enough that they outweigh the differences in my opinion. And the similarities for righteous living is much better for humans, so maybe they all come from a common source, for which we have diluted, and that one source is known as God!

The similarities of the Eastern and Western religions all teach that one must first develop the inner self by transforming to a higher consciousness. If we develop the inner self with good or godly traits, then the outer or physical self will become better. This inner self development will not only help our personal life, but our neighbors as well. We must purge the fleshly desires to selfishly compete with others to become artificially and materialistically complete. The inner self or soul cannot be satisfied with selfish acts of pleasure, wealth, power, fame, etc. The more the flesh gets, the more it wants. These fleshly objects will ultimately lead to particular acts of self-destruction, such as hatred, jealousy, war, envy, extreme pleasures, etc. Buddhism, Confucianism, Hinduism, and Taoism, all warn against these selfish and fleshly acts to please the inner self. To be one with God is to be one with your true self.

One may ask, just what is our true self? Huston Smith, in his book *World's Religions*, describes the true self in the Hindu tradition like this:

> The human self, and animating it, is a reservoir of being that never dies, is never exhausted, and is unrestricted in consciousness and bliss. This infinite center of every life, this hidden self or Atman, is no less than Brahman, the Godhead. (22)

This is described by Buddha another way, as noted from Huston Smith:

> Nirvana is the state in which the faggots of private desire have been consumed and everything that restricts the boundless life is exhausted. Affirmatively, it is that boundless life itself. (pp.77)

The inner self is eternal and infinite, but only good or godly endeavors will truly develop this life. The rationality is this, fleshly or selfish desire block and destroys the eternal inner self. Smith states it this way:

> ...In the Confucian scheme, the good man or woman is one who is always trying to become better. (pp.113)

A better life is what everyone wants.

> Pleasure, success, and duty are not what we really want, the Hindus say; what we really want is to be, to know, and to be happy. No one wants to die, to be in the dark about things, or to be miserable. Pleasure, success, and duty are only approximations of what we really want; they are apertures through which our true wants come through to us. (pp. 22)

In the Christian faith we find similar beliefs in *Luke 12:15* of the Holy Bible, Jesus says; "*Take heed, and beware of covetousness: for a man's life consisteth not in the abundance of the things which he possesseth.*" Jesus also states in John 10:10 that he came to give us life and it more abundantly. Through him our carnal desires are alleviated, and our eternal life or self begins to increase. A Christian begins to study to gain better knowledge, to seek that which is right and righteous, to become more like God, and our Savior. In the Holy Bible, *Romans 1:17* says; *"For therein is the righteousness of God revealed from faith to faith: as it is written, the just shall live by faith."*

What is the connection to it all, for your true self?
An emphasis should be placed on the need to become one with yourself, the need to be completely whole. When an individual seeks the spiritual part of their life, confidence builds from within the person. When confidence is built from within a person, inner joy is received and is expressed by the outer self. The person begins to see the outside world as spiritual extensions and their neighbors become a part of themselves. With that being said we can truly understand the Christian passage in the Holy Bible; *Thou shalt love thy neighbor as thyself. St. Matt. 19:19.* This statement becomes alive and fulfilling to know that God has given different people the same message, from different viewpoints. The joy is to understand that we are not restricted or limited to selfish acts of human nature, but we can obtain spiritual confidence to love everything and everybody; because the eternal you transcend the physical you, so the embracing of all humankind becomes possible.

The goal is to direct humans to become a complete person of righteousness and to be one with the eternal God. The message is to live a righteous life free from evil influence. To make all this happen, a person has to be truly willing to commit to the teachings and philosophies of the righteousness of God. If he or she is not committed, then all we have remaining is a masterfully written script composed into ancient books. The righteous teaching religions of the world, serve a tremendous purpose for people seeking a righteous service. God's wisdom knows no boundaries, has no limits, and has no faults, so who are we to judge. The Eternal One can use any person, anything, or any religion if God so choose, to fulfill the fullness of time. If we totally reject the righteous path, the world becomes full of fatalistic spirits, which corrupts, steal, kill, and destroy.

The Christian faith teaches: *"...by the mercies of God, that ye present your bodies a living sacrifice, holy, acceptable unto God, which is your reasonable service. And be not conformed to this world: but be ye transformed by the renewing of your mind, that ye may prove what is that good, and acceptable, and perfect, will of God." Romans 12: 1, 2 of the Holy Bible.* So just like in the similarities of the Eastern philosophies, the total person can be one with itself, by changing the fleshly thoughts to one of spiritual thought.

6

TOLSTOY CHURCH AND STATE

"The church with a sense of community has a clear understanding of its place within the world. It knows itself and it knows the community."

Howard E. Anderson, Sr., 2003

What are you thinking about?

God's nature is far beyond the scope of anything humankind can imagine. Humans cannot comprehend total perfection, beauty, and righteousness as God does. To truly behold our universe and our world, in total hallow perfection, humans must be totally predicated to submitting of our minds. Actually the child's mind, uncluttered with human improvising, can better behold the glory of God. In the Holy Bible we can find these words in Isaiah 55:8,9; *For my thoughts are not your thoughts, neither are your ways my ways, saith the Lord. For as the heavens are higher than the earth, so are my ways higher than yours ways, and my thoughts than your thoughts.* The thoughts and ways of God, as written in Holy Scriptures, are the nature of God. The thoughts and ways of humans, as written in our history, are the nature of humankind. If humanity cannot think and act as God does, we will not be able to comprehend God's nature, for God's nature is holy. The actions of God are for deliverance and liberation, and our actions have been of deceit and deception. In no way can the unholy manufacture any essence of holiness.

As humanity has sought to build our civilizations through centuries past, we have shown our true nature. Our thoughts have been on gaining physical perfection and not spiritual perfection. Our actions have been toward physical violence to bring about change and civil togetherness. We have sought ways to think faster, jump higher, and become stronger, to obtain the humanistic form of perfection, but the only true nature of humans, as a whole, is that we have become more centered in selfishness. The human race has used military and police forces to move people from one area to another, to gain an advantage for one race of people over another. The outcome has been more wars, ethnic cleansing, and mass destruction. Humanity's nature as a whole has become more violent and God's nature is becoming less and less evident in our lives. Is there a way to keep humanity from being violent and to reach total perfection toward our neighbor?

God has given humanity the keys to become a more perfect creature, throughout our existence, in the form of religious writings and thought. We on the other hand have used the most harmful ways to govern ourselves in our cities, our nations, and even our religious institutions. In Leo Tolstoy's book, *The Kingdom of God Is Within You,* he addresses the questions of humankind's violent nature, and also searches for answers to, total perfection with our neighbor. He builds his argument on human violence and civil perfection from the view point of Christian thought, verses secular thought. Tolstoy brings the reader into his idea of mass nonresistance to evil slowly and methodically, to gain the reader's confidence to accept his thoughts without question.

This thirst for power and riches is only an interlude for war. Those who think their army is more powerful will not hesitate to use them. We can also see that whole economic societies have been built around this premise.

The book, functions as one in a series of arguments that Tolstoy directed against the Christian Orthodoxy of Russia during his time. He included response letters from American Quakers expressing their sympathy for his views on unlawfulness of Christian war and use of force of any kind. Tolstoy used inserts from African

American writers in his book also. The son of William Lloyd Garrison wrote to Tolstoy stating that he read his book on nonresistance to evil by force. Garrison concluded that he found ideas similar to those expressed by his father in the year 1838. Garrison's son also sent Tolstoy a declaration or proclamation of nonresistance drawn up by his father nearly fifty years before Tolstoy. It is exciting to know that a century before Martin Luther King Jr.'s nonviolent resistance protest, during the Civil Rights movement, there was first William Lloyd Garrison the champion of the emancipation of African slaves.

Christian leaders meeting evil face to face, to keep our human sanity, for today.

The method of nonresistance to evil, expressed by the Quakers and Garrison, is heavily fortified by Tolstoy's own beliefs and ideas. One idea is that governments breed and encourage war with large standing armies. Tolstoy suggests that governments, which should have the people in mind who elected or appointed them, only set themselves up for more power and riches. This thirst for power and riches is only an interlude for war. Those who think their army is more powerful will not hesitate to use them. We can also see that whole economic societies have been built around this premise.

In his book, *The Kingdom of God is within You,* Tolstoy also suggests that the Christian church has benefited from the same philosophy. Not that the Church has consciously sought to start wars around the world, but by the support of the government has helped the church (pp148). Tolstoy's stance is Christianity, when governed by God's principles and laws cannot give total allegiance to any entity that is in violation with God's governing power. This stance is agreeable and the Church must be mindful not to trust in any evil or unjust government. But we must put some type of governing body in place, because the world as a whole is set on destruction and not on God's principles, so some type of governing authority is needed on earth. The church or religious institutions should never support any political figure or government blindly, and we should always denounce evil governments anywhere in the world.

The disarmament of a nation is an admirable idea, only if all nations disarm, but no way can the Christian nations disarm to be total at the mercy of other nations. There are greedy and power hungry people in power around the world and whole nations believing in terrorism to achieve their objective.

There are some good points about governments, as well as bad points, and the church has to be mindful of that fact. Churches and religious institutions everywhere have to stand for the good of all humankind and not show blind loyalty to its governing body, both inside and outside their organizations. Tolstoy says that the Christian church has gone against one principle of God, namely do not murder, as one example. He says when church officials show allegiance to government, and government believes in war, we commit murder. Tolstoy says that war is "Systematic Murder". (pp128, 129) So if God denounces murder, then church officials should denounce war and any government which relies on war as a means for existence. The denunciation of war is admirable, and a beginning in seeking world peace. Each religion of righteousness should influence their people and governments with great vigor to try and achieve this peace. Our efforts must be a collective effort by all religions, and not just Christianity or the philosophy will never work. Tolstoy's idea on war denunciation is a great beginning and only that, if all nations agree, but his idea of disarmament by Christian nations may be misguided.

The disarmament of a nation is an admirable idea, only if all nations disarm, but no way can the Christian nations disarm to be total at the mercy of other nations. There are greedy and power hungry people in power around the world and whole nations believing in terrorism to achieve their objective. We must have an armed force to defend against aggression. That is not to say that we should build an entire economic structure based on war items either. No nation should be centered on weapons and large standing armies, this philosophy can only lead to war, because if one has a lot of weapons at some point the weapons will be used.

An aggressive military based nation feeds into the violent nature of humankind. As a Christian we should be against the violent nature of ourselves, and we cannot depend totally on weapons, for God is our total dependence, but as a Christian nation we reserve the right to defend ourselves. Christians or any righteous religion, cannot allow nations or governments with weapons of mass destruction to have free will to do as they please either. Take a page out of Nazi Germany under the reign of Adolf Hitler. His regime attempted genocide of an entire race of people, and this would include too large a loss of a number of Christians. So it is a little disturbing to read in Tolstoy's book, this statement; "Until our warriors are disarmed and our armies disbanded, we have not the right to call ourselves a Christian nation." (127)

A Christian or any other religious believer in righteousness should never be heavily dependent on arms in the attempt to achieve goals by force. To disarm an entire nation, Christian or otherwise, cannot fit all situations. Even the Holy Bible does not speak about the disarmament of a nation as a practice, but the Holy Bible speaks against the dependence on arms instead of depending on God.

There is a situation in the Bible, just before Jesus was crucified. Priest and soldiers came to take Christ by force. Peter wanted to protect Jesus, took his sword and cut the ear off of a servant of the high priest. Jesus said, in Matt. 26:52; *Put up again thy sword into his place: for all they that take the sword shall perish with the sword.* Jesus was talking about a situation concerning one person, and not an entire race of people or nation. Jesus wanted Peter and the other disciples to be dependent on God and not the sword. Peter walked with Jesus and he carried a sword, because for him to put the sword up, he had to have it already. Jesus forced Peter and all those with them to focus on the situation at hand. When we read further, after Peter was told to put his sword up, in verse 53, Jesus said he could pray for more than twelve legions of angels for help.

Jesus knew he had plenty of help to save himself if he wanted it, but his main purpose was to bring, all who would believe, into spiritual perfection. So Jesus chose not to use force to obtain his objective, but the ability to use force was ever present. Good must be ready to combat evil by any means necessary, but good's main objective to achieve peace should not be force of arms. The main focus must be righteousness, holiness, and liberation. Jesus wants humanity to receive this Godly truth, for the nature of God is the essence of holiness.

Why we as humans can not solely trust in ourselves.
What is the nature of God? The Holy Bible instructs us that God is love, long-suffering, patient, kind, righteous,

and faithful. If our world is to survive for another two or three centuries, the human nature can no longer be opposite the nature of God. We cannot afford to let our governments and nations be opposite the nature of God either. Throughout human history there have been too many wars, crusades, evil rebellions, and massive ethnic cleansing, in the name of god and country, to last through eternity. All cultures and races must absorb the true nature of God for all our sakes and that true nature is of love.

Tolstoy also believed that the only help for humankind is the nature of God. He believed that humanity could not love humanity alone, apart from the love for God, because without the love of God, in his book *The Kingdom of God is within You,* Tolstoy says "There is no motive to produce it." (107). The human nature is opposite God's nature, meaning we are selfish, unloving, neurotic, and impatient. When that nature is forced upon family, nation, and state, how can any outsider, be totally accepted without the love of God? So thus we push and fight, compete and combat, sometimes for no apparent reason. The question is this, is our true nature one forced on us by outside sources? Most religions teach that humans are inherently good creatures of God, born in a sinful world, and influentially except sin by outside sources.

Tolstoy warns the church not to allow outside sources such as governments and rulers of the state to force their will on the church. True believers of God must not blindly be in alliance with the governments, but give allegiance to God. When we, the church, better ourselves for righteousness sake, then we can influence governments and states for righteousness; we in turn can produce a better world in which to live.

Tolstoy also warns the Christian church of its role in accepting the elitist way of life, that the elite classes, alone with governments, have enslaved people around the world as workers. This enslavement causes hatred, animosity, and jealousy, which in turn will lead to fighting of some sort. He urges the people and governing church officials to emerge themselves into all the principles of God, and to leave the outside influence where they permeate alone. But as Christians and law abiding citizens, we must continue to seek out those representatives for justice and righteousness. Tolstoy made great points for justice in his writings, because he was an influence to Mohandas Gandhi of India, who created a theory of nonviolent resistance for India's independence of British inequality, completed in 1948. Gandhi was an influence on Martin Luther King Jr., who championed the U.S. Civil Rights Movement for racial equality.

So what is next for us to do?
The governments of the world have caused many problems to be inflicted upon the many people that they

govern. The paradox is we need governments, because there are so many unruly people of the world who believe in nothing else but unruliness, so something is needed to maintain civil order. The question has been asked before: *Why has God allowed evil things to happen in our world?* God has given us the correct path to follow, but humans always try to do things as we feel within ourselves. We disregard the righteous religious teachings of the world for anything which seems logical and will fit our own nature. The limited knowledge of the future by humans, can only bring a greater destruction based on our past, and to try to create a future based on our present, only limits a greater righteous future. Tolstoy believes strongly in dismantling armies, especially by Christian nations, but the author has disregarded the violent past histories of all humankind over the world. He speaks as though every person on the planet is Christian by nature, but, every person is not Christian.

Humankind, as a whole, has not even learned from the past, when it comes to wars, totalitarianism, and attempted genocide. Think about these examples as a course of human nature. The Romans conquered the vast majority of the ancient world powers, so Napoleon tried to duplicate the process with France against all of Europe. What the Nazi power structure attempted by using ethnic cleansing and genocide, the Serbians tried a similar tactic on the Kosovians in the mid-1990s.

What our history shows as a whole is the lack of a benevolent godly nature for our nations, and instead, a recurrence of aggressive violent nature repeatedly duplicated century after century.

In this new millennium, it is an understatement to say that people are wondering what is in store for all of humankind. One thing is for sure, people will keep their present nature unless we allow the Hallowed Omniscient to make a change. The dismantling of armies is a noble idea, but all nations must comply in order for the idea to be righteous for all. Let us not forget Napoleon, Adolf Hitler, Saddam Hussein, Hideki Tojo, and others like them, because these type of people also manipulate the people they govern, and their religious institutions, to do as they please.

We cannot let evil or misguided people manipulate our churches and religious organizations. A stance for righteousness must be the focus, and to be righteous in our thoughts and mannerism should be our main goal. To be a Christian does not mean we have to dismantle our armies, because there are too many evil thinking leaders among us around the world. As believers in God's nature and principles, we cannot be totally dependent on our armies or governments either, because as world citizens, we must understand that this planet is all we have to live on, and respecting every world citizen is essential. In retrospect, having faith that God will guide us in all our affairs and help us to make the right decisions is the beginning for world peace. With our limited foresight of the future and our embracing of wrong past histories, unless we change humanities' violent nature for God's benevolent nature, ARMAGEDDON will be humanities to behold!

7

THE TIME HAS COME

"If the moral community is not limited to people in one place, neither is it limited to people at any one time. Whether people will be affected by our actions now or in the future is irrelevant. Our obligation is to consider all their interests equally."

James Rachels, 2010

Whose set of principles and methods are you dependent on?

In our modern society we have produced a set of rules or principles that are deemed rules of ethics. These ethical principles are produced to create a sense of peace and structure in the work place, and also in established organizational institutions. But ethics without some type of authority to enforce her principles will not stand on its own. We humans have proven throughout history we do not have the wisdom to enforce anything fairly for each individual. Sometimes our selfish ambitions and predetermine goals cloud our decisions for other people. So peace and harmony continues to elude us as a whole. With one person at a time seeking peace within themselves, through the spirit of God, only then can the world obtain peace. The foundation has already been laid by holy principles and moral laws the world over, sanction by an Omnipotent God. God is the supreme authority by which these holy principles can maintain balance in every person's life. This is done by God's Holy Spirit examining the motive and intent of the individual's heart. Some people may call this examination our conscious, but I prefer to call it the super natural presence of God!

The time has come to take hold of the super natural, for the sake of peace. We already know the consequences of our past historical options and actions, none have brought us closer to that peaceful goal. As a whole, humans have not learned how to think and decide righteously, and understand the consequences of our decision making thought process. What we do at the present moment, can affect our future, but never change a decision in the past. The past decision is always forever ready to affect the present, so we can learn how to make righteous decisions for our future.

The time has come for us to stop trusting in our own natural abilities and start trusting in the super natural principles of God for human life. The super natural principles of God are the written word of God recorded in the scriptures, of the major religions the world over. Righteous living is the only way for humanity to create a lasting relationship with each other. Think about the possibilities of everyone wanting to live by an unselfish mannerism. We have the ability to comprehend and obtain this purposeful way of life, but we must focus in on the righteous life and not be distracted by the non-righteous. The non-righteous living of greed, selfishness, jealousy, animosity, and hate, only destroys life. Righteous living of grace, sharing, joy, peace, and love, will increase life for all kind. The righteous way of living is not an unrealistic way of thinking; humans as a whole just refuse to accept it. We need the righteous way of life to totally influence the unrighteous way and not vice versa.

The Omnipotent God has the last say to it all in any way you believe. Jesus said in Matt.13:47-49 in the Holy Bible: *Again, the kingdom of heaven is like unto a net, that was cast into the sea, and gathered of every kind. Which, when it was full, they drew to shore, and sat down, and gathered the good into vessels, but cast the bad away. So shall it be at the end of the world; the angels shall come forth, and sever the wicked from among the just.*

*All humans are taught to be one way or another from birth,
so we have the ability to change.*

Can you really believe one culture is historically superior to the next one?

The time has come to stop the agitating and archaic superiority mode of thinking, where one race of people believe they are superior over another or one human superior over another. But rather let us think on how we can help someone better themselves and grow, without them feeling like an inferior person. Each race, throughout the centuries has made major contributions to our existence, and each human can make a positive contribution; if we only try the righteous and not be programmed with the non-righteous thinking. All humans are taught to be one way or another from birth, so we have the ability to change. We have already been using the non-righteous thinking on the world population, and the superiority complex has only created a negative atmosphere for all kind. When one believes they are totally superior to the environment, the environment gets destroyed. When one believes they are totally superior to another human being, they will not accept another person's ideas. When one believes their race is totally superior to another race, it creates a dangerous ethnocentric view. Even when one believes their religion is totally superior to another, they will force their religion upon another. God never forces the God self upon humans, we must accept God willingly. I have willing accept my belief and so have others in their belief, and I cannot be changed from my belief and probably neither can they be changed. We need to focus on what is the most important for all and that is righteousness overcoming evil; the good overcoming the bad.

It is my desire that we would stop masking God. What is meant by masking God is when we as humans create God in our own likeness and image. When we create God to look like one human over another or one race over another, all our human shortcomings get involved. There are some humans who will not accept the principles of God because we created God in drawings and paintings, to look like a certain race. Which is contrary to a principle found in the Holy Bible: *Thou shalt not make unto thee any graven image, or any likeness that is in heaven above or that is in the earth beneath, or that is in the water under the earth. Exodus 20:4.*

Humans have a tendency to mistrust anything, or anybody that is different from themselves and their briefs. The difference could be language or knowledge, in some cases the difference is merely a method of teaching. Although the information and the outcome for life are nearly identical to our own, we still try to discredit their writings and ideology for ours; thus creating despair and complexity like a ball of confusion.

We have masked God into many religions around the world based on ourselves, intensifying the confusion. So through the centuries confusion has created wars and fighting for the wrong reasons and we all know who the author of confusion is, that being the devil. We know the devil wants to promote and execute destruction of human life, hatred, lawlessness, and ungodly principles. God wants to unite and liberate all humans for righteousness sake, but we have pitted one religion of righteous living against another, instead of being against evil. If a religion that is promoting and exercising peace, love, harmony, and understanding, then who am I to be radically involved in trying to dismantle that religion. So I will believe in my religion and you yours and in the end of things God will do the separation.

The time has come to stop the national, racial, global, and religious fighting. Humans have too much to gain and nothing to lose by stopping barbaric behavior. The human race can become so much stronger by just learning how to create a better world for all humans to live in. We have built a technological advanced society and by no means are all of our advances bad for our environment either. But our world can be so much better than it is now and without imposing on, or destroying other cultures. The problem is, we have let the non-righteous and the non-righteous way of living and thinking dominate our world, through different types of leaderships with their influences, based on fast results. In the book, *Developing the Leader Within You*, John C. Maxwell makes his observation this way:

> …I concluded that each one of us is both influencing and being influenced by others. That means that all of us are leading in some areas, while in other areas we are being led. No one is excluded from being a leader or a follower. Realizing your potential as a leader is your responsibility. In any given situation with any given group there is a prominent influencer. This influencer may change with a different group of people or a different situation to become one of those influenced by another influencer. (pp2)

We can become better in our society and live united only if we can put a side our petty differences. The time has come to embrace God. By embracing the word of God and the principles of God, we ultimately embrace the God Self, the spirit of God. If humanity keeps on doing what we have done for centuries, the time will come for God to do what must be done according to scripture to bring humanity to our original state of being. In the Holy Bible, Rev. 21: 1- 4 states: *And I saw a new heaven and a new earth: for the first heaven and the first earth were passed away; and there was no more sea. And I John saw the holy city, New Jerusalem, coming down from God out of heaven, prepared as a bride adorned for her husband. And I heard a great voice out of heaven saying, Behold, the tabernacle of God is with men, and he will dwell with them, and they shall be his people, and God himself shall be with them, and be their God. And God shall wipe away all tears from their eyes; and there shall be no more death, neither sorrow, nor crying, neither shall there be any more pain: for the former things are passed away.*

There is an all-powerful being, who is everywhere at the same time, with all knowledge, and is the provider of the universe. Since God is God and God does what God wishes to do, let us follow God's righteous principles, and live an enriched life. There are many pathways in life, some are good and some are bad. Some pathways are great ones and some are dangerous. The fact of the matter is this; God is always trying to lead us down a path that will keep us in his perfect will. For a human life is a very precious gift of God.

For too long we have neglected life and taken our lives for granted. We are special, we are unique, and we should treat each other that way. That special life is what the Holy Bible is trying to convey to us all, so let us celebrate life by worshiping the giver of life thru Jesus the Christ is my belief.

We can become better in our society and live united only if we can put a side our petty differences. The time has come

to embrace God. By embracing the word of God and the principles of God, we ultimately embrace the God Self, the spirit of God.

So the message I want to convey to everyone that read this book is this: the time has come for us to stop letting the super-rich of the world continue to control our lives with their money and influence. They sit on different corporations governing boards with their controlling stock interests; they give large sums of money to the endowment of education, and donate money to the social networking to the poor and the building of religious institutions all for control of the masses. The goal is to put and keep us all in slavery and bondage to them the world over, so we fight one another, create wars against one another, and in hate kill one another, while the super-rich continue to get richer and gain more power over us all. Because they know that there a two things that all religions of the world agree on is, (1st) all religions of the world except financial offerings completely, (2nd) all religions except the devil or evil as their enemy without bias, so the super-rich keep the masses blind and confused to the two completely.

As a Christian I say to everyone we all know who the author of confusion is and it is that influence which is behind the scenes controlling all the ills of our world. So to those who deem themselves to truly strive for righteousness regardless of religion, we must unite to combat unrighteousness and do what is truly right toward each other to stump out hatred, racism, and slavery the world over. Our mission is to help make humanity better by the commission of the almighty God, not to start wars and create mass genocide.

So I believe the answer to the question, "Does morality depend on religion?" is no. Morality does not depend on religion, because a religion can be formed from any or a number of things and that religion may not be governed by a set of truly holy principles of right and righteousness. Morality, in my opinion, is a set of non-destructive rules or principles, that are deemed holy, with its base core remaining a constant, but has flexibility in its application and base on a personal point of view of morality. In other words, an individual's morality can differ from another's based on a person personal moral construct view point.

So any religion or moral construct without the ancient holy and righteous principles of Holiness (such as the Ten Commandments) I believe is not valid. God is the supreme authority by which these holy principles can maintain balance in a person's life, by examining the motive or intent of the individual heart. Some people will call this balance our conscious, and even modern ethics without some type of authority to enforce her principles will not stand in our modern age. Whatever you choose to be your form of religion and you do not have a set of morally holy principles to govern it, is doom to chaos and confusion which will lead people down a path of destruction. So if you can't see or understand God as being God the "Supreme One", then see God as the Super Natural Being, who implemented the natural laws of life: the Theory of Natural Law you may say. The Almighty does not want to prevent humanity from creating on our own accord, but the Omniscient of God reserves the right to guide our thoughts on the use of our creations to protect and make positive changes for our planet and humanity. **What direction will we take?**

REFERENCES

Chapter One

Longman III, T. (2013). *The Baker Illustrated Bible Dictionary.* Grand Rapids, MI: Baker Books.

Scofield, C. (1967). *The New Scofield Study Bible KJV.* New York, NY: Oxford University Press, Inc.

Chapter Two

Britannica., T. N. (15th Edition). *The New Encyclopedia Britannica.* Encyclopedia Britannica Inc. Founded 1768.

Carpenter, E. (1920). *Pagan and Christian Creeds.* New York: Harcourt, Brace, and Co.

Fischer, K. (1990). *Reclaiming the Connections: A Contemporary Spirituality.* Kansas City: Sheed and Ward.

Jackson, J. G. (1972). *Man, God, and Civilization.* Secaucus: Citadel Press.

Longman III, T. (2013). *The Baker Illustrated Bible Dictionary.* Grand Rapids, MI: Baker Books.

Scofield, C. (1967). *The New Scofield Study Bible KJV.* New York, NY: Oxford University Press, Inc.

Smith, H. (1994). *The Illustrated World's Religions: A Guide To Our Wisdom Traditions.* New York: HarperCollins Publishers.

Thomas, M. (1978 4th printing). *The Silent Life.* New York: Farrar, Straus, and Giroux.

(1984). *Webster's New World Dictionary.* New York: Warner Books.

Chapter Three

Crooks, Robert & Baur, Karla. (2014). *Our Sexuality, 12th Edition.* Belmont, CA: Wadsworth Cengage Learning.

Jackson, J. G. (1972). *Man, God, and Civilization.* Secaucus: Citadel Press.

Norwich, J. o. (1982). *Revelations of Divine Love.* Harrisburg: Morehouse Publishing.

Rhys, J. (1945). *Shaken Creeds: The Virgin Birth Doctrine.* London: Watts & Co. .

Scofield, C. (1967). *The New Scofield Study Bible KJV.* New York, NY: Oxford University Press, Inc.

Smith, H. (1994). *The Illustrated World's Religions: A Guide To Our Wisdom Traditions.* New York: HarperCollins Publishers.

Chapter Four

Fischer, K. (1990). *Reclaiming the Connections: A Contemporary Spirituality.* Kansas City: Sheed and Ward.

Scofield, C. (1967). *The New Scofield Study Bible KJV.* New York, NY: Oxford University Press, Inc.

Chapter Five

Corey, G. (2009). *Theory and Practice of Counseling and Psychotherapy, Eight Edition.* Belmont: Brooks/Cole, Cengage Learning.

Scofield, C. (1967). *The New Scofield Study Bible KJV.* New York, NY: Oxford University Press, Inc.

Smith, H. (1994). *The Illustrated World's Religions: A Guide To Our Wisdom Traditions.* New York: HarperCollins Publishers.

Chapter Six

Anderson, S. H. (2003). *Growth Principles for an Exciting Church.* DeSoto: Alpha Books.

Scofield, C. (1967). *The New Scofield Study Bible KJV.* New York, NY: Oxford University Press, Inc.

Tolstoy, L. (1984). *The Kingdom of God Is Within You.* New York (Originally): University of Nebraska Press.

Chapter Seven

Maxwell, J. C. (1993). *Developing the Leader Within You.* Nashville: Thomas Nelson, Inc.

Rachels, James; Rachels, Stuart. (2010). *The Elements of Moral Philosophy, Sixth Edition.* New York: McGraw-Hill.

Scofield, C. (1967). *The New Scofield Study Bible KJV.* New York, NY: Oxford University Press, Inc.

Made in the USA
San Bernardino, CA
30 September 2015